Pausing
with a
Poem

Pausing with a *Poem*

Magic in the Air

Claire-Louise Price

Copyright © 2025 Claire-Louise Price

The moral right of the author has been asserted.

Apart from any fair dealing for the purposes of research or private study, or criticism or review, as permitted under the Copyright, Designs and Patents Act 1988, this publication may only be reproduced, stored or transmitted, in any form or by any means, with the prior permission in writing of the publishers, or in the case of reprographic reproduction in accordance with the terms of licences issued by the Copyright Licensing Agency. Enquiries concerning reproduction outside those terms should be sent to the publishers.

The manufacturer's authorised representative in the EU for product safety is Authorised Rep Compliance Ltd, 71 Lower Baggot Street, Dublin D02 P593 Ireland (www.arccompliance.com).

Troubador Publishing Ltd
Unit E2 Airfield Business Park
Harrison Road, Market Harborough
Leicestershire LE16 7UL
Tel: 0116 279 2299
Email: books@troubador.co.uk
Web: www.troubador.co.uk

ISBN 978-1-83628-448-2

British Library Cataloguing in Publication Data.
A catalogue record for this book is available from the British Library.

Printed and bound in Great Britain by 4edge Limited
Typeset in 11pt Adobe Garamond Pro by Troubador Publishing Ltd, Leicester, UK

*To my dog Polly,
who magically came into our lives
at just the right time*

(see 'The Story of Polly')

Contents

Introduction	ix
Inspiration	1
Christ Church Oxford 5.30pm	2
Aldeburgh seafront 4.17pm	3
Sitting outside a café in St Giles	4
Lesson not learned	6
The Unknown Warrior	7
Aftermath	8
At the Summit	9
Glacier	10
Tea at Dyneley House	12
Tapestry	13
Heart of Oak	14
Act of Courage	15
Wings I The Robin	16
Wings II The Butterfly	17
The Story of Polly	18
Keep Mum	20
Milestone	21
Out of Reach	22
Healing Tears	23
Valentine's Day	24
Rosé	25

Lament of the Christmas Trees	26
Office Politics	28
A Handful of Haikus	29
Keep in Line!	30
Dandelion's Deadline	31
Magic Golf	34
Lesson Learned	36
Where's Whitsun?	37
Coronations	38
Fifth Dimension	40
Acknowledgements	43
About the Author	44
Also by the Author	45
Review Quotes	46

Introduction

In these poems I have attempted to observe, capture or celebrate moments of magic in everyday life. We don't always notice them for they are often invisible, and if we do sense them, we don't always have time to reflect on their significance. Sometimes they originate from thoughts, opinions, personal qualities, historic vibes or spiritual essences, often they cannot be explained.

In this book I invite you to sit down with a cup of coffee (or tea!) and share some of these moments with me. A pause is sometimes all that is needed to draw the magic that happens every day into our daily lives.

Most of the poems are inspired by an experience but a few are drawn from my imagination. For example, 'The Unknown Warrior' is imagined, as is 'Lament of the Christmas Trees'.

There are two sonnets, one is Shakespearean and the other is Petrarchan. If you are wondering, the difference between the two forms is in the rhyme scheme. 'Keep Mum', the Shakespearean sonnet is, I am glad to say, an imagined story, whereas 'The Story of Polly' (the Petrarchan sonnet) is true.

The poems about Oxford and Aldeburgh capture magical moments at a precise time. The pair of 'Wings' poems celebrate natural phenomena that I actually witnessed.

The 'magic' of political power and its effects are observed in 'Lesson not Learned', 'Office Politics' and 'Keep in Line'. The haiku 'War Virus' has been described as "savage in its irony". Alternatively, you might like the Matterhorn's speech about climate change in the poem 'At the Summit'.

The final poem 'Fifth Dimension' is a faithful description of St Peter Mistail, a church located in a remote canton of Switzerland. It is not the building, but the unseen dimension within, which is perhaps the most powerful example of hope and benevolence in the whole collection. Our visit was all the more magical because the discovery was completely unexpected.

I hope you enjoy your moment of reflection with one of the poems in this book. If you do, please write and let me know which is your favourite. As always, I would love to hear from you.

Warmly,
Claire-Louise

Facebook: @poetryclp   email: price.clairelouise@gmail.com
                              www.inspiringwriting.co.uk

Christ Church Oxford 5.30pm

The scent of freshly fallen rain
on soaking sandstone, luscious lawns.
Droplets of stories washed from walls,
pooling in flagstones, chalices of history
hollowed by student footsteps over centuries.
In deserted cloisters
cracks in ancient arches
slowly drip mysteries
into
freshly
fallen
rain.

Inspiration

Magic happens every day
if you keep your eyes open
your senses aware
your belief unflinching
in the face of rational thinking.
You can feel it, follow it
live it, love it,
marvel at it.
Oh hello! There you are…
and you begin to write.

Aldeburgh seafront 4.17pm

November twilight.
I climb the grassy bank and there's the sea
An intense full Moon
Low in the sky, surveys the darkening deep.

Her fiery counterpart had cast warm rays
on agitated waves that afternoon.
Now Artemis Moon shoots a silvered path
Over smooth water, earthing at my feet.

The Moon waits motionless, serene,
observes the scene, before ascending
into dove grey evening cloud,
well satisfied with her masterpiece.

Sitting outside a café in St Giles

Daubs of red all around
Red parked car
Red pillar box
Red poppy wreaths

Wooden sign nearby, swinging in the breeze
Army
Be the Best.
At what? Getting killed?

Spatters of red on young men
Red bobble hat
Red woollen scarf
Red canvas bag

Groups of students
Passing by, laughing.
How I miss the banter
Now my sons have left home.

Streaks of yellow move and flow
Yellow double decker bus
Yellow rays of sunlight
Yellow knee high boots

Cheer up.
Remember, they may have flown the nest
But they never had to
Go to war.

Lesson not learned

History knocks on the door
not once, not twice, but thrice or more.
Many lessons, will we learn?
No, the bad times will return.
We did not want another war
and yet it's happened like before.
A thumping sound of soldiers' feet
in the country, in the street.
They march with hope, not knowing fear
until reality is near.
'Peace' is an ignored refrain
while politicians seek to blame
each other, sacrificing men
and futile fighting starts again.

The Unknown Warrior

Do not DNA me
Do not find out my name
If it's ever known, then life
Will never be the same.

By robbing me of mystery
Thousands will lose hope
That I might be their family
Their only way to cope.

So many fell, were never found
Husbands, sons or brothers
They lie beneath a foreign ground
With friends and faithful lovers.

Yet here I lie in greatest state
Full in the public glare.
While poppies frame my resting place
This story I will share:

I still remember clearly the words of my dear gran
On the day I was seven, when the clock struck eleven
She looked at me so piercingly
And said – 'Cometh the hour, cometh the man.'

Aftermath

Waterfowl Lake
Is devoid of ducks.
No animals lurk behind trees
No need to stop for bears on the highway
Or elk. Or moose.
No birds of prey wheeling over the mountains
No birds in flight. Anywhere.
No people in the next town
People, animals, all have fled,
Fled the devastating wildfire.

At the Summit

Good afternoon. My name is Matterhorn.
I'm representing Earth in human form.
Something's up: I lost my snow today.
That should not happen till the month of May.
I asked the North and South Poles, no debate
their ice is melting at a faster rate.
The oceans East and West do both agree
their currents have got warmer than the sea.
The rivers are reporting they must flood
then cover towns and villages with mud.
The deserts sent a message: 'We are spreading
too far, too fast, we don't know where we're heading'.
The forests are all clustering in fear
of fires, now starting any time of year.
Trade winds have dropped, and with their final breath
are heralding our planetary death.
If humans do not act now I must warn
soon all that's left will be the Matterhorn.

Glacier

Ice trapped for thousands of years
Reaches the end of eternity.
Sheer drop into the fjord
Calves into the waiting water
with a boom like thunder,
floats and gradually melts
into salinity.
Fresh water is finally free
Returns to the sea.
What is death
but another form of life?

Tea at Dyneley House

Mary and Maggie and Mabel
Sat down for tea in a group
They chatted and smiled
And grew kind of wild –
The cook had put Love in the soup!

Tapestry

         will not last forever.
One day a thread   loosens
   then an interlocked stitch is   lost
producing a hole   quickly mended.
A central piece of the pattern later
                            disappears
Leaving a   gaping   heart-shaped   void.
Over time, the edges of the mesh
   shrink inwards while
more holes appear overnight in the diminished unravelling
work

Now there is only one thing to be done:
Choose your brightest, rarest,
most expensive threads or wools,
the ones you kept too long for best –
zany orange, youthful yellow, rebel red
entwine with purple, green and white
and with gnarled, yet nimble fingers
work in half cross, tent or basket stitch,
defiantly refreshing the faded canvas
combining a riot of colours until they shine
brilliantly upon a tiny stage.

Heart of Oak

He goes stoically without
fuss in the early hours. We young
striplings sadly watch his
inevitable
demise. A death rattle
reverberates as he
topples slowly on to yielding ground.
Noble to the last, he waited
clung on with
unstable roots until it was
safe to let go.
Children, dogs, walkers
               tucked up in bed
               unaware of giant
               boughs unsustained,
               overloaded with foliage. He needed to
                        fall.
            Now he lies in state
            we mourn his loss
            in silence.
                    Two hundred years
                    of majesty
                    await the
                    dawn chainsaw.

Act of Courage

'I can't do it!'
 'Yes you can, can, can'
'I won't do it!'
 'Yet you must, must, must'
'I won't survive it!'
 'Yes you will, will, will'
'The fire's getting closer!'
 'You must jump, jump, jump'
'The firemen won't catch me
 When I fall, fall, fall!'
'I am going to push you
 So you leap, leap, leap.
Now you are in safety
I'm still high, high, high
I'm paralysed by fear
But I must try, try, try!
I do not want
I do not want
I do not want
to die.

Wings I The Robin

On the spur of the moment
I picked up my bag
put a lead on the dog
and ran for the next train
along the narrow path
wondering -
Do I need to go right now?
Could it wait another day?
It's a long journey.
To my surprise
the robin perched upon the fence
did not take cover in the bushes
as he usually did when people passed by.
Instead he flew alongside me
all the way to the station
perching on the wire fence
waiting for me to catch up
then flying ahead again.
I had my answer there and then
and got there in time.

Wings II   The Butterfly

It was sixty years ago
but I've tracked you down.
You are here somewhere
under the small lawn by this church.
I hesitate. No tiny gravestones left.
A Peacock butterfly appears.
Auburn wings with bright blue dots,
lifespan of eleven months,
alights upon the grass, stays very still.
Now I know where to scatter
pink rose petals from my garden.

The Story of Polly

She came into our lives one snowy day
A little puppy, curly haired and white
My husband went to hospital that night
Too late to change our minds, she had to stay.
By luck, by grace, by magic some might say
She never whimpered, never even whined
As if she knew why she was left behind
A guardian angel when he passed away.

When I first met her on the Isle of Dogs
An eight week old delightful bichon frise
Enthusiastic, climbed upon my knees.
We bonded through unspoken dialogues.
Now twelve, in all these years of widowhood
She's been a fun companion. Done me good.

Keep Mum

I had not seen the little girl for weeks.
She scanned the crowded square to try and find
me, standing by a weeping willow tree,
then ran towards me, leaving Dad behind.
She looked so sweet and happy, dressed in pink,
and hugged me with the warmth of a young child
quite unaware what passers by might think
while I, too old to care, bent down and smiled.
'Oh Nana what's the matter? Please don't cry!'
She didn't know the reason for my tears
She'll never know the history of why
the truth will be suppressed for many years.
Her stalwart, loving Dad brought her to stay
a while with me. Her Mum had run away.

Milestone

Mismatched holdalls stuffed with clothes
carrier bags overflowing with trainers and socks
boxes of carefully packed computer games
a single volume from the reading list chucked on top

A taut teenager
a fraught household
we all needed space.

My husband piles it all from hall to car
no room for me; a hasty change of plan.
I thought this milestone would be more momentous.
An endured kiss on the cheek, a farewell grunt to his brothers,
barely a wave from the passenger seat
and he's off.

Out of Reach

Two thirsty travellers in the desert
run towards a
pink haze full of promise,
an oasis full of tempting fruits.
Parched, they try to drink
drops of juice that
evaporate on the tongue.
Coconuts lay on the ground, they
break them open
revealing empty husks.
Deceived, they
watch the haze recede.
The oasis has no substance.
It is a mirage in the sands.

Healing Tears

I can't cry now
people would see
I must suffer
silently

I won't cry now
where would we be?
Keep it from
the family

I do cry now
but then I see
I've acted too
courageously

'I'll cry more now
say what I feel
my tears will fall
and then I'll heal.

Valentine's Day

Bubbles wink
playfully upwards
from the base
of the champagne glass.

Happy memories
cause pockets of grief
long hidden, to float
gently to the surface.

Red rosebuds on the table
Softly say 'Take heart.
Love will unfold again.'
We blink back tears.

Rosé

She fancied white wine
he lusted after red,
they agreed on rosé.
A new label on the wine list.
Highly recommended sir, madam.
We'll go for it.
Fabulous with her fish,
delicious with his duck.
She enjoyed the tingle of ice cubes
he preferred it smooth and straight.
The art of compromise
is the key to success.
Fifty two years of marriage
and still going strong.

Lament of the Christmas Trees

We are celebrated, feted
brilliantly baubled
spangled with tinsel
with fairy lights festooned.

Stripped three weeks later
brutally discarded
onto unforgiving pavements
we lie naked. Marooned.

Pedestrians walk round us
while we await the truck
like corpses for the plague cart
face down in the muck.

Pine needles scattered
like hopes dashed and shattered
as if we never mattered
inert, helpless, stuck.

Some of us stand upright
propped against a gate
hanging on to dignity.
Others lie prostrate.

Yet despite the devastation
This truth we have learned:
One day we will regenerate
One day we will return.

Office Politics

I am merry
You are sozzled
He is drunk

I'm concerned
You are anxious
He's in a funk

I'm articulate
You are wordy
He writes junk

I'm strategic
You're backstabbing
He is sunk

I stepped back
You went absent
He's done a bunk

He smelled a rat
You're a rodent
I'm a skunk.

A Handful of Haikus

Unknown Warrior
Soldier, rest in peace
represent thousands of dead
your final orders

Paris
to find romance look
up at river and skyline
pavements are grubby

Line count
hard to achieve when
six stanzas get redrafted
into a haiku

Rheims 1940
vintage crop is safe.
bombs burst like champagne bubbles
they can't reach the vaults

War Virus
Pandemic's over.
Hurrah! Now we can resume
killing each other

Keep in Line!

Regimentation implementation
Is the order of the day
We're squeezing out the slack
Let's cheer, hip hip hooray!

Automatons produced
In every primary school
We're sticking to the Plan
Don't you realise, you fool?

The kids will learn that testing
Is the most important game
Stress is all that matters
Creativity is lame

Imagine is a dirty word
Insightful is no better
Do not use your instinct
The rule book, to the letter!

Regimentation implementation
Not creativity and wit
Just follow the instructions
Our words will never fit.

Dandelion's Deadline

The mower stopped a few feet short of me
the lawn was shorn of dandelions and weeds
the gardener went inside to have his tea
my puffball was intact with all its seeds.
Titania's message hid within, for she
had asked me for some help with pressing needs.
How to transmit her pleas to Oberon?
A few more minutes and I would be gone.

No breeze to blow it to the nearby wood
where Oberon was gathering his arms
to fight the Queen in battle, if he could
but stay protected from her fairy charms.
He knew the fight would really be no good
for any fairy, this would do them harm
and yet his pride forbade a softer stance.
He'd had enough and given a last chance.

I despaired of carrying out my mission
Grey thunderclouds were darkening the sky
I had no time to make a wrong decision
'Please help!' I begged a passing butterfly.
I gave him his instructions with precision
'OK' he said 'I'll carry it, I'll try.'
He flew off and by great good fairy luck
he found, and gave the message, straight to Puck.

Puck sought an audience with the fairy King
and whispered the Queen's words into his ear
their sweetness made his heart and senses sing
then all his pride and anger disappeared.
He called his courtiers to a council ring
declaring that her fairies need not fear.
No war was fought. The King and Queen again
ruled fairyland. And me? Saved – by the rain.

Magic Golf

I whacked a golf ball
Way up high
It went beyond
The clouds and sky

Through outer space
Right to the Moon
I yelled at it
'Please come back soon!'

The golf ball landed
In a crater
The Moon called back
'I'll find it later!'

Nothing happened
Until that night
A whizzing sound
Gave me a fright

Through the window
Above my head
Something landed
On my bed

A chocolate orange
My favourite treat!
How did it get there?
That was neat

The Moon called out
'My work is done
I've just lobbed back
A hole in one!'

Lesson Learned

Intuition said *Don't go!* but I did
Or I would lose a thousand quid.
Travel insurance's terms and conditions
Do not accommodate gut intuitions.
I fly as planned to Tenerife.
It starts off well then morphs into grief.
During the night I get symptoms of flu.
Sore throat itchy eyes. What shall I do?
I make a decision to rearrange travel,
then fly home that day before plans unravel.
Next morning I waken in my own bed
Alarmed by the buzzing noise hurting my head
I cannot get up, my temperature's high.
Thank goodness I got home while I could still fly.
I told you so, said my intuition. I knew all along.
Next time I will listen.

Where's Whitsun?

The feast of Pentecost got lost
became Late May Bank Holiday
so Whitsuntide like Larkin's brides
receded into memory

'Exam season' was the reason
the date must stay the same
'Standardise so kids revise
let Whitsun change its name!'

This dubious claim was first explained
in nineteen sixty seven
A pact, and then the Banking Act
consigned the day to Heaven.

Coronations

Whither do you go, Archbishop?
  whither do you go?

To crown a Sovereign, my friend
  to crown a Sovereign

Why do you humbly walk, Archbishop?
  why do you humbly walk?

The greatness is not mine, my friend
  the greatness is not mine

And are you not afraid Archbishop?
  are you not afraid?

The Lord is walking with me too
  believe me, I have prayed

What if you drop the crown, Archbishop?
  what if you drop the crown?

If I dropped the crown, my friend
  their world won't tumble down

I will anoint with holy oil
   the Monarch's head and chest

The crown can only symbolise.
   The *oil* is where God's power lies.

Fifth Dimension

No road leads there.
Only a narrow pilgrim path
winds past a meadow
full of alpine flowers
until you reach
the ancient church
set in rural heaven.

No photo, no painting,
no image can capture
the hush
of ten centuries of prayer.

Faded frescoes grace
white walls reflecting light.
Altars hewn from rock stand
in a trinity of apses.
In their centre shines a candle.
No words, no signs
to busy the mind.
Only profound silence.

Acknowledgements

Heartfelt thanks to my loyal friends, to my inspiring Oxford tutors and impressive course colleagues, and especially to my son Rob and my goddaughter Louisa. I could not have written this book without all your interest and unwavering support. Thank you.

About the Author

Claire-Louise's career was in journalism and communications for national charities. She worked freelance for a few years after her husband was diagnosed with a terminal illness.

She has written three poetry books about her widow's journey from grief to serenity. Often light hearted and always profound, the poems have helped and inspired many readers.

'Pausing with a Poem', Claire-Louise's fourth collection, does not focus on widowhood, although it is mentioned in the wonderful story of Polly.

She never intended to become a poet and thinks this is why she can help people find their own poetic voice. As a volunteer guide, she was recently invited by Westminster Abbey to be 'Poet in Residence' for a day, encouraging pilgrims and members of the Abbey's community to find their inner poet.

Claire-Louise has three adult sons and four grandchildren, and loves writing, travelling and dancing.

Also by the Author

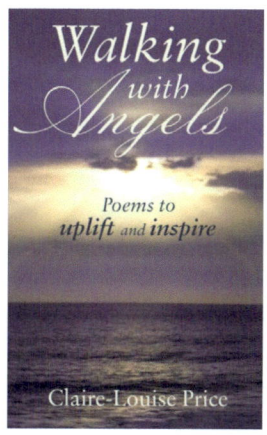

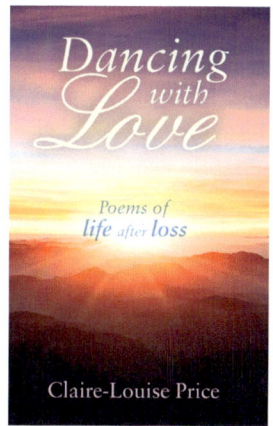

Review Quotes for 'Pausing with a Poem'

Claire-Louise is a sharp-eyed, sympathetic observer of the details and practice of everyday life. Her readers will enjoy these poems immensely.

Claire Crowther, poet

Concise, precise and life-affirming, Claire-Louise's poems go straight to the heart of what it is to be human in a busy world.

Joanna Miller, author of 'The Eights'

Review Quotes for the Angels trilogy:

'This book is a joy'   *Woman & Home* magazine on *Walking with Angels*

'Open this book at any page and you will find something to escape into for a moment, or longer'

Amazon reviewer on *Dancing with Love*

'I loved this accomplished and assured third poetry collection. Humour, reflection, wry observation – it is all there.'

Frances Gibb, author and journalist on *Living with Joy*